Rain Rain Rain Rain Rain Rain Rain Rain Rain Rain Rain Rain Rain Rain Rain Rain Rain Rain Rain Rain

Rain

by
Robert Kalan
illustrated by
Donald Crews

GREENWILLOW BOOKS
A Division of William Morrow & Company, Inc.
New York

Text copyright © 1978 by Robert Kalan
Illustrations copyright © 1978 by
Donald Crews and Robert Kalan
All rights reserved. No part of this book
may be reproduced or utilized in any form
or by any means, electronic or mechanical,
including photocopying, recording or by
any information storage and retrieval
system, without permission in writing
from the Publisher. Inquiries should
be addressed to Greenwillow Books,
1350 Avenue of the Americas,
New York, NY 10019.
Printed in the United States of America

22 21 20 19 18 17 16 15 14 13 12

Library of Congress
Cataloging in Publication Data
Kalan, Robert. Rain.
Summary: Brief text and illustrations
describe a rain storm.
1. Rain and rainfall—Juvenile literature.
[1. Rain and rainfall] I. Crews, Donald.
II. Title. QC924.7.K34 551.5'781
77-25312 ISBN 0-688-80139-0
ISBN 0-688-84139-2 lib. bdg.

With love to my parents
R. K.

. . . and to mine
D. C.

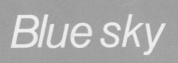
Blue sky

Yellow sun

White clouds

Gray clouds

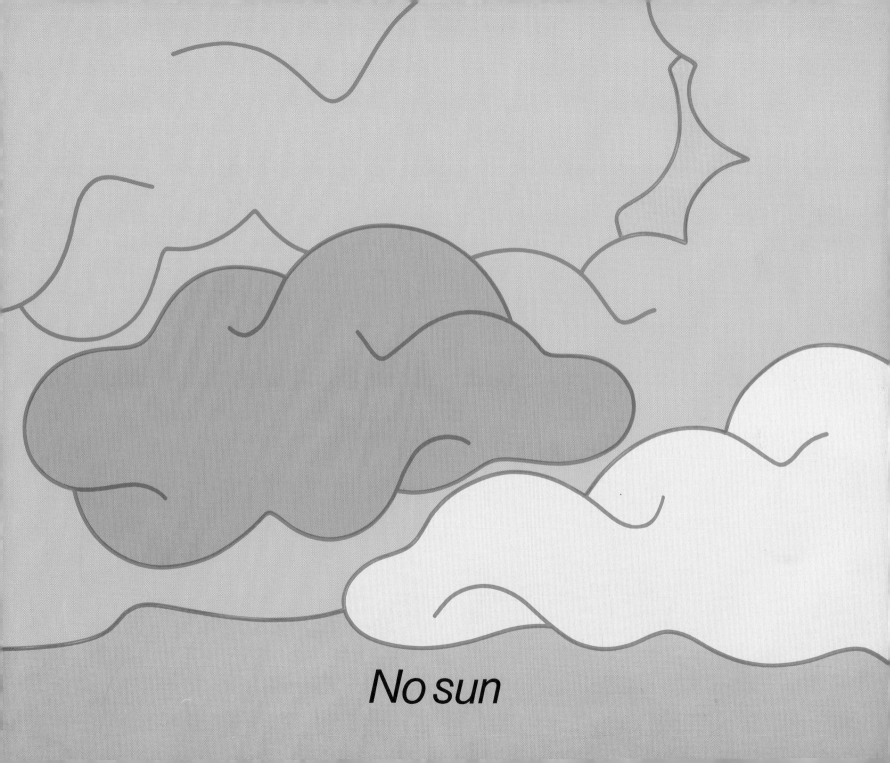

No sun

RainRainRainRain
RainRainRainRain
RainRainRainRain
RainRainRainRain
RainRainRainRain
RainRainRainRain

Gray sky

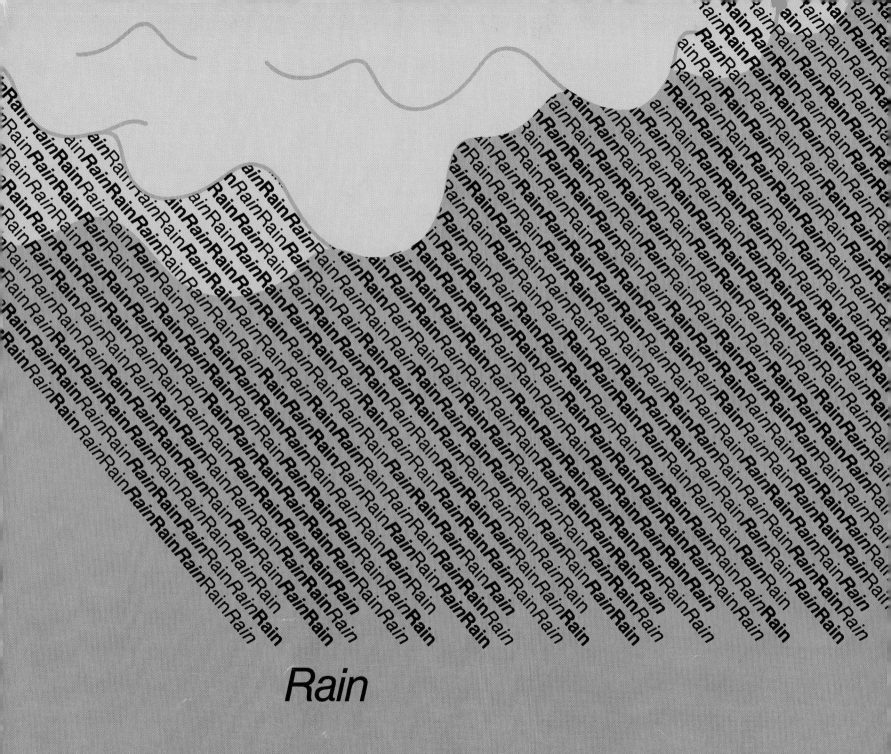

Rain

Rain on the green grass

Rain on the black road

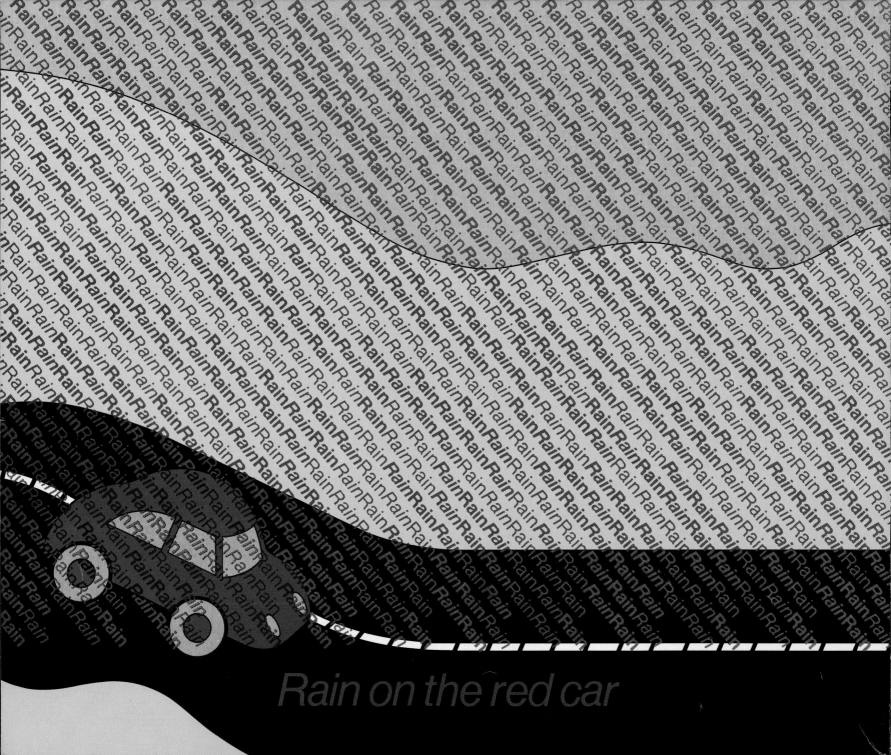

Rain on the red car

Rain on the orange flowers

Rain on the brown fence

Rain on the purple flowers

Rain on the white house

Rain on the green trees

Rain

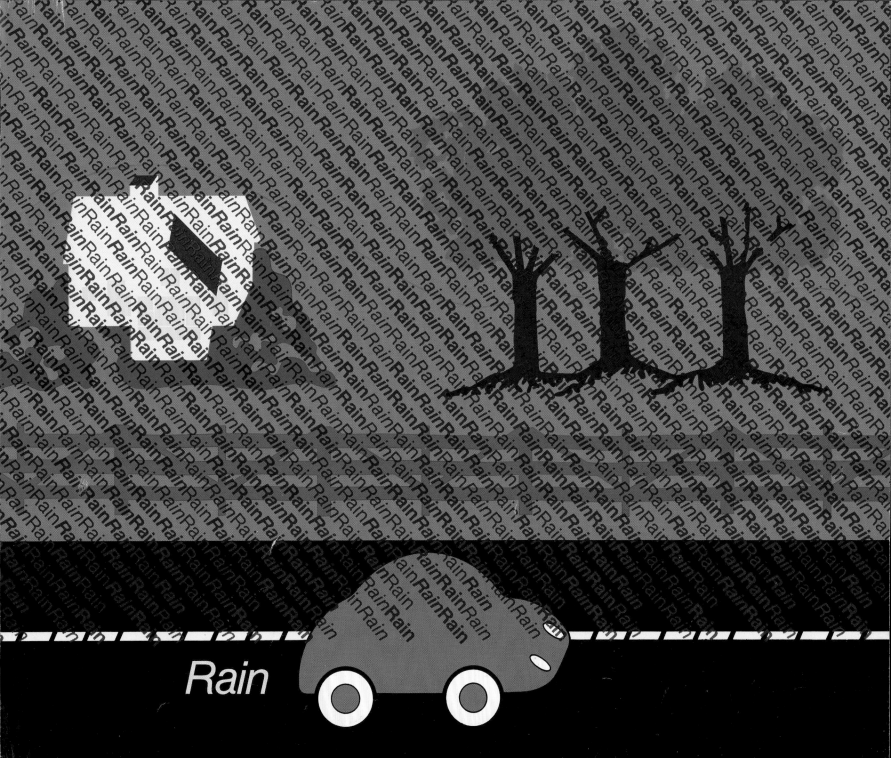

Rain

RAINBOW

ROBERT KALAN was born in Los Angeles. He was graduated from Claremont Men's College.
He has taught reading to both gifted and remedial students as well as kindergarten and fourth grade, and completed a master's degree in education at Claremont Graduate School. He is currently living in Seattle, where he teaches a course in writing for children at the University of Washington.

DONALD CREWS was graduated from Cooper Union for the Advancement of Science and Art in New York City. He has written and illustrated many books for young children, including We Read: A to Z and Ten Black Dots. He and his wife Ann are freelance artists and designers, and live in New York with their two daughters.